Explore Space!

# Space Shuttles

by Gregory L. Vogt

**Consultant:**
James Gerard
Aerospace Education Specialist
NASA Aerospace Education Services Program

# Bridgestone Books
an imprint of Capstone Press
Mankato, Minnesota

Bridgestone Books are published by Capstone Press
151 Good Counsel Drive, P.O. Box 669, Mankato, Minnesota 56002
http://www.capstone-press.com

*Library of Congress Cataloging-in-Publication Data*
Vogt, Gregory.
    Space shuttles/by Gregory L. Vogt
    p. cm.—(Explore space!)
    Includes bibliographical references and index.
    Summary: Explains how space shuttles work and how astronauts live and
work in them.
    ISBN 0-7368-0200-2
    1. Space shuttles—Juvenile literature. [1. Space shuttles.] I. Title. II. Series: Vogt, Gregory.
Explore space!
TL795.515.V64   1999
629.44'1—DC21                                                                98-45664
                                                                                          CIP
                                                                                          AC

**Editorial Credits**
Rebecca Glaser, editor; Steve Christensen, cover designer and illustrator;
  Kimberly Danger, photo researcher

**Photo Credits**
NASA, 4, 8, 10, 12, 14, 16, 18, 20
Tom Stack & Associates, cover, 6–7

2  3  4  5  6  04  03  02  01  00

# Table of Contents

orbiter

## Space Shuttle Lift-Off

Space shuttles are vehicles that carry astronauts into space. Large engines and rockets power space shuttles. Astronauts ride in the orbiter section of space shuttles. Astronauts arrive in space only 10 minutes after lift-off.

**orbiter**
the airplane-like part of a space shuttle where astronauts ride

5

**payload bay (closed)**

**solid rocket booster**

**main engines**

**USA**

**thrusters**

**external fuel tank**

**flight deck**

## Power

A space shuttle needs a lot of power to blast into space. The brown external tank holds engine fuel. This fuel gives power to the main engines. Astronauts control three main engines from the flight deck. Two solid rocket boosters give a shuttle extra power during lift-off. Smaller engines called thrusters help change a shuttle's speed in space.

solid rocket
booster

## Solid Rocket Boosters

Two solid rocket boosters give a space shuttle thrust. The boosters fall to the ocean two minutes after lift-off. Workers will clean and fix the empty boosters. Then they will refill them for the next flight.

**thrust**
the force produced by a rocket engine; space shuttles need the thrust of solid rocket boosters to leave Earth and enter space.

## External Tank

The brown external tank outside the orbiter holds fuel. The fuel lasts about nine minutes. Astronauts separate the empty tank from the shuttle. This makes the shuttle lighter and easier to fly. The external tank breaks into pieces as it falls. Only the orbiter continues into space.

## Crew Cabin

The crew cabin in the orbiter has two areas. These areas are the flight deck and the middeck. The pilot and the commander fly the orbiter from the flight deck. The astronauts live, eat, and sleep in the middeck.

## Eating in Space

Astronauts prepare food and eat in the middeck. They add water to dried food and heat it in an oven. Astronauts can eat upside down in space because everything floats. Astronauts do not feel gravity in space.

**gravity**
the force that pulls things to Earth

satellite

payload
bay

USA

## Satellites

The payload bay sometimes holds satellites. Astronauts use a robot arm to put satellites into orbit. Some satellites take pictures of Earth. Some receive signals from Earth and send signals to Earth. These signals can be telephone calls or TV shows.

**orbit**
the path an object follows while circling a planet; the pull of Earth's gravity keeps an object in orbit.

17

## Experiments in Space

The payload bay sometimes holds large laboratories. Astronauts do experiments there to test new ideas. Astronauts try to learn how animals and plants grow without gravity.

## Return to Earth

Astronauts use the thrusters to slow down the orbiter. Gravity pulls it back to Earth. Astronauts land the shuttle like an airplane. A parachute slows the shuttle. The astronauts climb out of the orbiter after it stops. They tell scientists on Earth about the space mission.

**space mission**
a special job or task in space; a mission may be a science experiment or putting a satellite into orbit.

21

# Hands On: How Orbits Work

Space shuttles circle Earth when they fly in space. The path they take is called an orbit. You can see how an orbit works.

<u>What You Need</u>
Jump rope
An adult
A child

<u>What You Do</u>
1. Have the adult stand in the middle of an open room.
2. The adult holds one end of the jump rope. The adult is the Earth.
3. The child holds the other end of the jump rope. The child is the space shuttle.
4. The child should walk in a straight line while holding on to the rope. The rope will force the child to walk in a circle.
5. The adult should slowly rotate in place. The adult should pull the rope in when facing to the left and to the right to create an oval-shaped orbit.

The rope represents gravity. The path the child walks is the orbit. This activity shows how gravity pulls an object to keep it in orbit.

# Words to Know

**orbit** (OR-bit)—the path an object follows while circling a planet; the pull of Earth's gravity keeps an object in orbit.

**orbiter** (OR-bit-ur)—the airplane-like part of the space shuttle where astronauts ride

**parachute** (PA-ruh-shoot)—a large piece of strong, light cloth joined to an object; a shuttle's parachute slows it down when it lands.

**payload bay** (PAY-lohd BAY)—the place in the back of the space shuttle that holds satellites and science laboratories

**satellite** (SAT-uh-lite)—a machine that circles Earth; satellites take pictures or send telephone calls and TV programs.

# Read More

**Branley, Franklyn Mansfield.** *Floating in Space.* New York: HarperCollins Publishers, 1998.

**Deedrick, Tami.** *Astronauts.* Community Helpers. Mankato, Minn.: Bridgestone Books, 1998.

**Kallen, Stuart A.** *Space Shuttles.* Giant Leaps. Edina, Minn.: Abdo & Daughters, 1996.

# Internet Sites

**Canadian Space Agency—Kool Zone**
http://www.space.gc.ca/ENG/Kool_Zone/menu.html
**NASA Space Shuttle Virtual Tour**
http://www.ksc.nasa.gov/shuttle/missions/sts-90/vrtour/
**Starchild: The Space Shuttle**
http://xte.gsfc.nasa.gov/docs/StarChild/space_level1/
  shuttle.html

# Index